You Just Have To Laugh Publishing

First published in the USA in 2006 by
You Just Have to Laugh Publishing
Lenexa, Kansas 66215 U.S.A.
youjusthavetolaugh.com or naster.com
Printed in Korea by asianprinting.com

2 4 6 8 10 9 7 5 3 1

First Printing: 1998 March
Second printing: 1998 October
Third Printing: 2000 complete revision
Fourth Printing: 2006 complete revision
Fourth Printing: 2006 complete revision
Fifth Printing: 2009 partial revision
Library of Congress Catalog Number: 2006901964
ISBN: 0966314565

Guidebook design:
Nancy Loughlin and David Naster
Cover photos: Isaac Alongi

Contents

FEAR

As children, most of us are brainwashed into believing that laughing at tough times is bad. We are taught humor is an inappropriate response to illness, injury, danger and grief. Instead of teaching children that laughing out loud is sometimes bad manners, we scare them into thinking humor itself is wrong.

That's tragic. When we teach children that laughter is bad, we rob them of one of life's most vital survival skills — humorous thought.

It's ironic. We teach kids not to laugh because we are afraid people will think we are bad parents. But a truly bad parent crushes a child's playful spirit out of insecurity and fear.

David Naster

IT'S ALL IN MY THINKING

I have been getting on stage, making people laugh since I was 12 years old. Forty years later, I still sometimes get scared before performing.

Here's what I do: I convince myself the audience won't like me. I don't trust my comedy. I panic.

Now, when this happens, I recognize and stop my fearful thinking. I think how much I love making people laugh. My comedy has worked hundreds of times. My message is strong — humor and laughing helps people. Once my negative thought turns positive, my fear is gone.

I'd always heard people are as happy as they choose to be. I didn't get it. After creating this guidebook, I do: I create fear. I create happiness. It's all in how I think and what I do.

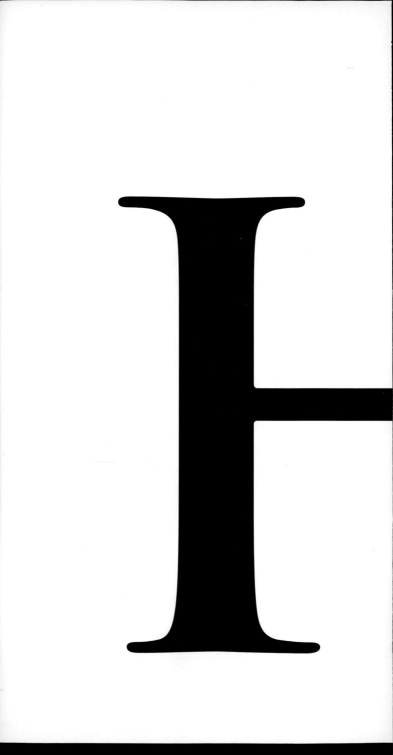

NO ONE ESCAPES TOUGH TIMES

Illness
Injury
Danger
Grief

- Their mere presence produces fear.

- Fear does not create tough times — your response to fear does.

- How you *act* or *react* to fear determines how *tough* illness, injury, danger and grief will be.

Acting is good — it protects.
Reacting is bad — it paralyzes.

A Category 5 hurricane is approaching your city.

Act — Get out of there to protect yourself from illness, injury and death.

React — Stay there, worrying about what might happen.

Your child is diagnosed with cancer.

Act — Do everything possible to save your child.

React — Let depression keep you from getting your child effective medical care

Positive Action

Richard Bloch was diagnosed with lung cancer. Doctors gave him 90 days. Richard kept a positive attitude, finding new ways to laugh everyday.

Richard, "A doctor at the National Cancer Institute told me about a female patient who showed what a negative attitude can do. The woman thought she was doomed, even though her cancer was treatable. In fact, the doctors said she was certain to survive if she followed the treatments. The patient still insisted she was doomed.

"At her autopsy, they found no living cancer cells in her body. It was like she willed herself to die."

Richard survived over 25 years using humor.

Acting produces well-being.
Reacting creates misery.

HUMOR

acts positive on fear.

Like fear, humor exists in our thinking. We have all heard the expression: "A SENSE OF HUMOR." There is no such thing as a "sense of humor." A "sense of humor" does NOT exist.

The five senses are physical — sight, hearing, taste, touch and smell.

HUMOR is not a "sense." It is a learned way of thinking. A MIND-SET.

Having a "sense of humor" really means the intellectual ability to find absurdity.

Example — a cartoon

You see the picture on the screen and hear the sound effects, but it doesn't become funny until you intellectually register absurdity — a coyote with a rocket on his back trying to catch a road runner.

* **If Wile E. Coyote had money to buy all that Acme stuff, why didn't he just buy dinner?**

More Absurdity:
1. Smoking areas in restaurants are like peeing areas in swimming pools.
2. It takes one careless match to start a forest fire, but a whole box to start a campfire.

Humor

created from a SET-UP

is followed by a PUNCH LINE

✓ The SET-UP is any word, phrase or situation to joke about.

A 65-year-old woman comes home from her annual physical check-up. She finds her husband sitting in his chair reading the paper.

She says, "Great news. The doctor told me I was in amazing shape. He even said I have the supple breasts of a 21-year-old.

Not looking up from the paper, the husband said, "Did he say anything about your ugly, fat 65-year-old ass?"

She said, "No. Your name never came up."

"Did he say anything about your ugly, fat 65-year-old ass?"

PUNCHLINE

"No.
Your name never came up."

✓ The Punch Line, written or said, is why we laugh.

How to create a Punch Line from the set-up:

1. distortion
2. word play
3. absurdity

example

(1.) DISTORTION

v to bend, twist, stretch, exaggerate

The room was filled with people in terrible pain. They were staring at the guest speaker, hoping he would have some magic cure for their suffering.

The speaker's topic:
How humor and laughter help patients deal with Level 10 back pain.

The speaker tells what happened:

"I started off with, 'Hi, I'm David and I'm an alcoholic. Oops, wrong meeting.'

"This brought surprisingly loud laughter. For the next 10 minutes, I hit them with my sure-fire funny stuff.

"Once I had them laughing, I asked the group to call out reasons why Level 10 pain is good.

The room fell silent. Everyone stared at me.

"After an a long, awkward pause, a man yelled, 'No responsibility!'

People laughed.

"A woman said, 'You get to sleep all day.' '"24-hour room service!"'another added.

More laughter

"Somebody called, 'More drugs!'

The room erupted.

"Voices grew louder as more got involved. People once frowning were laughing out loud. A woman in too much pain to sit up when the meeting started, was now perched on the edge of her chair.

"The biggest laugh of the day was when the oldest woman in the room said, 'The best thing about being at level 10 is that it is a better excuse than telling my husband I have a headache!'

The place went nuts.

"We did a quick check. Every person in that room had a lower pain level."

Distortion — a new perspective on reality

examples

(2.) Word Play

n using multiple meaning of words

Dick Shulte on surviving breast cancer: "My divorce was finalized on January 3rd. My mastectomy was on January 9th. I told people I lost three boobs in one week."

Kathy, "My brother had his legs and arms amputated because of diabetes. I started calling him my 'half-brother.' He loved it."

3. Absurdity

adj ridiculous, illogical, incongruous

Robert, "One morning, I was in bed and felt the pressure of a 100-lb. bag of rocks on my chest. A burning sensation shot up and down my left arm. I told my wife to call the doctor.

"Ten minutes later, the paramedics arrived. One of the guys had a mustache with about five hairs. The other acted like he had never worked a gurney before.

"While they were lifting me on the gurney, a wheel fell off. 'Mustache man' balanced the gurney while his partner crawled under the bed to retrieve the wheel.

"During this chaos, my wife was sitting on the bed, clutching the dog, singing, 'Nobody knows the trouble I've seen.'

"At the hospital, the paramedics couldn't find the ICU. The 'two stooges' argued as they tried every one of the building's floors.

"Eight days later, I woke up. I had suffered a heart attack. I'm not sure I would have survived if all of that crazy stuff hadn't distracted me. Now, when I remember my heart attack, I laugh."

PUNCH

LINES

from fearful set-ups –
make tough times better

Diane Strudwick, "I worked at a
hospital where a very troubled patient
jumped from the roof and died. That was not
funny.

"A few hours later, a nurse pointed out
that the man landed in front of a sign which
read: Patient Drop Off. That's funny."

Bill Mahoney found out he had cancer
of the bone, liver, pancreas, arms, head,
legs and back."

"I got cancer every place but my lungs,"
he said. "I'm sure glad I didn't quit smoking."

Dick Solowitz, "A man with Parkinson's
disease was delivering my father's
eulogy. As he read, his hands were shaking
so bad he messed up the names and
relations. This made my brother and I laugh.
I whispered. 'I want this guy for my funeral.'

"My brother shot back, 'You'd better go
before next Wednesday.'"

A SERIOUS QUESTION
(or two):

Why is it easy for some to find humor in tough times?
They already think funny.

Why is it harder for others?
They don't.

HOPE FOR THE FEARFUL

NO ONE IS BORN FUNNY. The ability to find humor is learned. Just as a good musician has to practice every day, anyone who wants to think funny has to work at it.

One way to practice is reading this guidebook. It has true stories of people acting on their fears with humor. Identifying *SET-UPS* in these examples will help you find *SET-UPS* in your own life. Recognize how distortion, word play and absurdity were used to create *PUNCH LINES*

Their examples will teach you how to make *PUNCH LINES* out of your tough times.

"Example is not another way to teach. It is the only way to teach."

— Albert Einstein

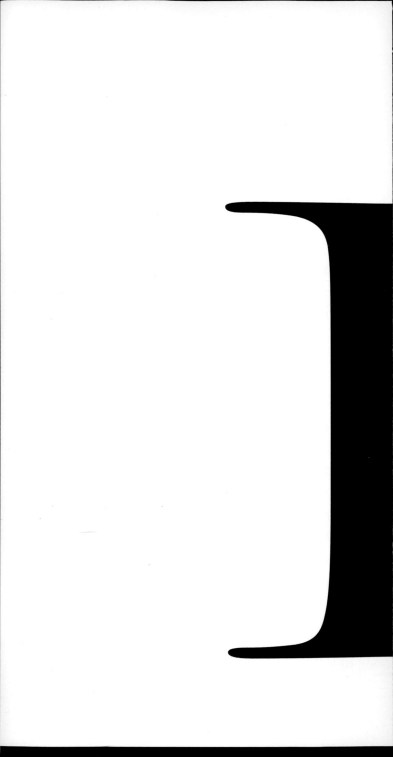

Illness

From the thoughts of
David Naster

Life deals some people a bad hand. Children are born with crippling illnesses. Deadly diseases strike the kindest souls.

The question to ask is not why bad things happen.

The question is, are you willing to find humor when they do?

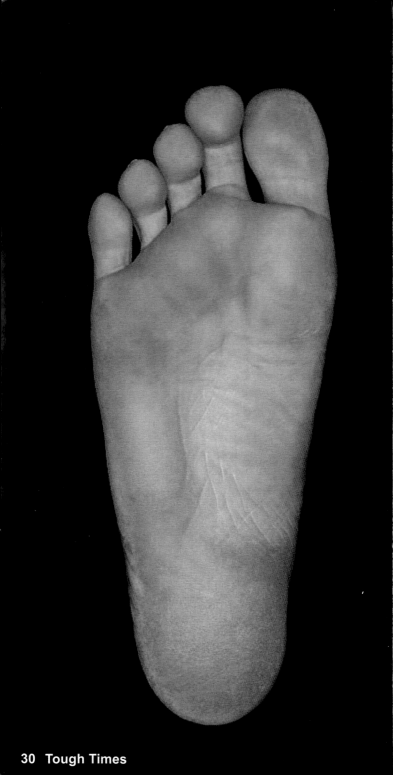

ABOUT A FOOT

A man wishing to
remain anonymous:

"I went to see one of my best friends
in the hospital. He had just had his
leg amputated. Walking into his room,
I was surprised to find him laughing
with a nurse.

"I said, 'How can you laugh at a time
like this?'

"My friend said, 'How can I not laugh.
Look at this card I just got.'

"The card read: 'Hope you get better
and get back on your feet.'

"The person who sent the card had
crossed out feet and written foot."

We're All Nuts

Mary appeared to have it all together.
She was upbeat, funny and outrageous.
She was a pillar of strength.
One day, she collapsed.

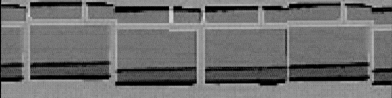

Mary, "I was committed. When they told me I was going to a mental ward, I cringed. But deep inside, I knew I needed to be there. One patient helped me get on the right track.

"I was depressed, eating in the lunchroom, alone. A guy I didn't know sat across from me. Without an introduction, he said, 'Look. You're nuts. I'm nuts. Everybody's nuts. We just got caught.'"

Born with Cerebral Palsy

Paul Shyrack, "I am a stand-up comedian. A stand-up comic stands and speaks clearly — neither of which I can do.

On stage in his wheelchair:

'I just broke up with my girlfriend. She pushed me too far.

'How many guys with CP does it take to screw in a light bulb?

'One ... but it takes 100 bulbs.'

"Comedy has taught me to laugh at myself. One day I could barely get out of my apartment because of snowy weather. I struggled, wheeling myself to the local coffee shop. Wet and cold, I finally rolled in the cafe. Everyone stared at me. I smiled and said, 'I feel sorry for those gimps that can't make it out today.'"

Paul's business card:
'If you can't understand me, drink more beer.'

Paul's promotional brochure:
'If people want to have a good time, I certainly won't stand in their way!'

PAUL SHYRACK

Perfect Vision

Kimberly Morrow, "Being born blind, I have always had the choice to laugh or get angry. I choose laughter.

"In college, whenever an instructor asked anyone to raise their hand if they couldn't see the projector, I always raised mine.

"When I became a teacher, I never told my students I was blind. I began class by saying, 'I'm Kimberly. This is my dog, Nadine. She barks once for passing notes and twice for cheating.'

"One time a young woman said, 'Ms. Morrow, I always raise my hand in class. How come you never notice me?'

"'There's a good reason for that, Sarah,' I said. 'I'm blind.'

"Humor makes my life more fun — like at check-out counters. Most cashiers don't notice I'm blind, even though I have a seeing-eye dog with me. When I pay by check the cashier always asks to see my driver's license.

"Smiling, I'll show my ID card. Then say, 'No, but you can see my guide dog's.'

"Another time, I was at an elegant restaurant with my date, Kevin. We decided on our selections. The waiter approached and talked like I wasn't even there. He asked Kevin, 'And what will she be having this evening?'

"'*She'd* like the filet mignon,' I said quickly. I love doing stuff like that — making fun of my blindness. Here's my favorite joke:

"'How does Helen Keller drive? One hand on the wheel and one hand on the road.'"

Shane Naster was born with McCune-Albright Syndrome. This rare disease turns bone into fibrous tissue. As a child he could run and play. Now, at 18 years old, he will never walk again.

Shane, "I have always had pain. I have it every day. There isn't an hour that goes by I don't. My legs and arms feel like they could break at any time. I have dreams about not having pain.

"Laughing helps my pain. Since people stare at me in my wheelchair, I like to wear a t-shirt that reads –

"Keep staring. I might do a trick."

Shane's school bus driver:
"Once, as I strapped Shane's chair down, his friend, Andre, got on the bus and said,

"'Hey Shane, get out of that chair. Everybody knows you can walk.'

"Shane didn't miss a beat.

"'Come on, Andre, take off that mask. You know it's not Halloween anymore.'

"The boys kept going.

"'Come on, Shane. We know you're a faker.'

"'Come on, Andre. You have to be better looking under that mask.'"

?????!?????!?????!?????!???

Sally Balot was worried she had Alzheimer's disease. She asked her grandson, Rich, to take her to the family doctor.

Rich, "At the doctor's office, grandma explained why she was afraid she was losing her memory — describing her symptoms.

"The doctor patiently sat and listened to grandma. After she finished talking, the doctor folded his hands, leaned across the table and said, 'You know what, Sally, I'd just forget about it.'

"Grandma and I were speechless. The doctor broke out into a huge smile. He assured us there was nothing to worry about.

"'Just forget about it' became grandma's ongoing joke."

?????!?????!?????!?????!???

Uncle Lou

Jerry Bressel, "My Uncle Lou has Alzheimer's. Father's Day, the family was gathered in the kitchen. One of the grand kids started singing *'Old McDonald Had a Farm.'*

"With every animal the kid sang, Uncle Lou made the sound of that animal, repeating the name. When the kid sang, 'on that farm he had some cows,' Uncle Lou would say 'cows,' and then make a long, drawn-out mooing sound.

"It was annoying.

"Every animal on Noah's Ark was mentioned. But Uncle Lou was enjoying himself, not doing any harm, so nothing was said.

"When the song finally ended, everyone applauded. The boy's aunt said, 'There sure were a lot of animals on Old McDonald's farm.'

"Uncle Lou slapped the table, stood up and hollered, 'It's his damn farm. He can have as many animals as he damn well pleases!'

"We laughed so hard, we had to pick ourselves up off the floor."

HUMOR IN BREAST CANCER

Barbara Johnson found losing her hair a great advantage:

Barbara, "My support group howled when I explained how I avoid long boarding lines at airports. As soon as the first-class passengers are called, I walk to the ticket agent, pull my wig off and say 'Chemo. Bad day.'"

No one ever stopped her.

A GREAT PAIR OF STORIES

Margaret:
"I went for a check-up after my mastectomy. As the doctor examined me I said, 'Since I only have one breast, I'm assuming I get 50% off of this visit.'"

Sunny:
"I was being wheeled off for a mastectomy. My husband and two daughters stood in the hall, looking scared.

"Pointing at them I said, 'I'll be right back. I've got to get something off my chest.'"

Frank Slater, "I was 61, my wife 58, when we got married. After our honeymoon, my new bride was diagnosed with bone cancer. Her doctor said she should not expect to outlive her friends.

"We immediately went out to find her new, *older* friends."

Jim O'Hara
Multiple Sclerosis
Patient

Jim, "A lot of funny things happen in the bathroom. Like the time I taught my friend, Howie, how to use a crane which helps me use the toilet. Swinging me through the air like a car engine, Howie burst out laughing.

"'Who else is going to do this, but your best friend?' Howie asked.

"'Okay, best friend,' I said, 'finish the job and wipe me.'

"Sometimes, my humor gets dark. Once, I told a doctor to cut off the body parts I can't use any more. At least I'd be lighter to lift. Now that's funny."

RULE On HUMOR

The doctor told **David Rule** he had a brain tumor.

David said, "I'm confused."

The doctor repeated, "David, you have a brain tumor."

David said, "I'm still confused."

The doctor, "What are you confused about?"

David said, "Don't you need a brain to have a brain tumor?"

The doctor didn't laugh. David did.

David, "The news was so absurd, I laughed. I guess I could have cried or lost it, but the doctor was so serious, I thought it was funny.

"From that moment, I refused to be in a room with anybody who wouldn't smile. I'm not into doom and gloom. Even though **I am serious about my recovery,** I have more confidence if the people taking care of me laugh.

"Some of the doctors had a hard time understanding my attitude. One asked mom if I understood the seriousness of a brain tumor.

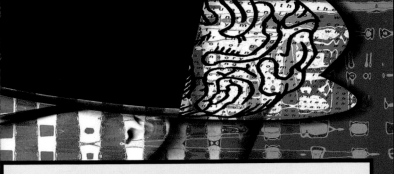

"Mom said, **'Oh, he understands. That's why he's laughing.'**

"Another person that fought my use of humor was my girlfriend. She said, 'You are in a grave situation. I will not come see you until you realize it. And I am not sure if I should even visit you at all because brain tumors are contagious.'

"I asked if she was serious. She was.

"In my spookiest voice I said, 'You better not come back, you might catch a brain tumor.'

"Before my first operation I was talking to a woman going in for open-heart surgery. Our medication had us both giggling. As they rolled her away, she said, 'See you on the other side.' I called back, 'Do you mean heaven or the recovery room?'

"She laughed all the way down the hall."

Twenty years after his first diagnosis, David got another brain tumor. David's mom said, "We have another fight on our hands."

David said, **"Get my gloves."**

David beat the second tumor, too.

Stu Swersie, "I have emphysema. Not just emphysema but EMPHYSEMA. I carefully cultivated this condition over a 40-year period, one tasty cigarette at a time.

"I have been told emphysema is terminal. Making the best of that prediction, I decided to enter the **Emphysema Olympics**.

"Looking over the application, I saw the usual events:

- 10-Yard Underwater Relay
- Four-Inch Speed Bump Jump
- Downhill Wheelchair Slalom
- Oxygen Tank Toss
- Balloon Blow-Ups

"Highlighting the games is the exciting Metric Mile Run, which starts Monday morning and finishes sometime Wednesday.

"These are exciting times. I can't wait for the games to begin.

"The thought of it leaves me breathless."

HANDY vs SMART

David Yonnley, "My wife, Tina, has Multiple Sclerosis. One summer she was having a dreadful day because of the heat. She was downright grouchy.

"Joe, our handyman, was doing some odd jobs for us. He is a great guy, good at what he does, but not the sharpest tool in the shed.

"After an argument with my wife, Joe pulled me aside and asked, 'Does Tina seem cranky today?'

"'Joe,' I said, 'that's the MS.'

"He nodded his head. 'I understand. My wife gets that way during her time of month, too.'

"When I told Tina what Joe said, she laughed so hard, she cried. It helped her have a better day."

Hard Time

Dixie Peterson, "Christie and I went to visit Becky in the maternity ward. She had a baby girl. While there, Julie, an acquaintance, came into the room. We asked what brought her to the hospital. Looking down she said, 'My husband Richard ... he ... um ... has an erection that won't go down. It's a reaction from his heart medicines.'

"We didn't know what to say except, 'Oh.'

"As soon as she left, we broke into hysterics.

"We imagined what to say if we visited Richard:

'What's *up*?'
'How *long* have you been here?'
'I bet it's *hard* lying in bed all day.'

"All of us agreed the perfect gift for a person in his condition would be a ring-toss game. Becky begged us to stop. Her stitches hurt from laughing.

"Just then, Julie came back and said Richard would like us to visit.

"'Oh no.'

"We went into Richard's room, being careful not to look at the area of his problem. We also knew that if we looked at each other, we'd lose it. So we looked only at his face and kept our visit short — no pun intended.

"Becky, Christie and I still laugh about that day. Recently, I got a ring-toss game in the mail.

"No note attached."

The Spirit of '76

John Schuler's grandmother was confined to a hospital bed. It was sad and difficult for his family to accept that her mind was no longer sharp. She would tell some pretty wild stories.

John, "Once, my sister and I were standing by grandma's bed while she told one of her tales. She said, 'I've been up all night. They're putting on a talent show here. We have to practice. I told them I wanted to go to bed, but they made me dance all night. I'm tired. But the show must go on.'

"My sister started crying, but I just played along with grandma's stories. Soon my sister was watching in amazement as grandma and I enjoyed ourselves.

"My family followed my lead. Instead of being sad about grandma's fanciful anecdotes, we simply enjoyed her and her wacky stories.

"In grandma's final year, she constantly crowed about being 76 years old. She would boast of being the 'Spirit of '76.' We played along with that, too. She was actually 77."

"You are going to die.

"You have two years, tops."

Holly Dodd, "That's the truth. I could be gone in two years, two weeks, maybe two minutes.

"Sarcoidosis produces nodules of lumps beneath the skin. I have extremely painful nodes on my lungs, eyes and skin.

"I never whine. I've learned that complaining makes people disappear. Since I had no intention of being alone, I decided to have fun.

"When people ask me how I feel, I say:

'How am I? How do you think I am? I'm in pain, you moron.'

'And, I am not sick, I am health challenged.

"Then I got breast cancer. I had fun with that, too. I told people I have 'poop in my boob.'

"Then I went out and bought some fake 'Billy-Bob' teeth.

"They looked disgustingly real.

"SHOWTIME.

"Before and after each of my chemo treatments, I told the nurse:

"'My mouth feels funny. My gums seem swollen and my teeth seem to be growing.'

"The nurse documented each complaint.

"After the seventh visit, she called me in her office. The nurse looked at my chart and read it aloud. While her eyes were on the chart, I put in the 'Billy-Bob' teeth. The nurse looked up, saw my mouth and screamed. Then laughing, she had me trick three more nurses.

"We decided to fool the doctor.

"The next week I was sitting in the examining room — 'Billy-Bob' teeth in place. In walks the doctor. He sat. As he read my chart, he never looked up at me. He sounded puzzled as he mumbled, 'Teeth seem to be growing. Tingling sensation. Gums swollen.'

"When he finally looked up and saw my fake teeth, he jumped three feet — stumbling into a cabinet.

"Once he recovered, he said:

"'We need to radiate those teeth and stick them in your armpit. That should take care of any lymph node problems. I would also suggest flossing more often.'"

John had diabetes. He had both legs removed. All but one finger remained on each of his hands. He never quit laughing.

While in his hospital bed, all of his monitors went crazy — beeping and flashing. The nurses ran into his room and asked what was going on. John said he and his wife were talking about sex.

Doug had his legs and all but two fingers amputated because of diabetes.

His best friend, "The disability company sent Doug a letter asking if he was really disabled. Doug had me take a picture of him with shorts on. We sent the picture to the insurance company with the caption: 'What do *you* think?'

"Another friend, Dave, is short. We've always teased him about his height. After Doug got his legs amputated, he called Dave and said, 'Hey, I just had my legs cut off and I'm still taller than you.'"

Glenn, a crusty old guy and getting grumpier by the day, had his leg amputated because of diabetes. His family bought him a prosthesis, but he refused to wear it.

Glenn and his son, Ralph, were sitting at the kitchen table arguing about Glenn's refusal to wear the prosthesis. Ralph's eight-year-old son walked in the room, noticed the fake leg on the table and said, "Hey grandpa, take your feet off the table. You know you're not supposed to do that."

Even grumpy Glenn laughed.

Soon after, he began wearing his prosthesis.

Julia begins, "My 52-year-old husband was diagnosed with prostate cancer. After surgery, his treatments consisted of large doses of female hormones. These are the same body chemicals that give women hot flashes and *mood swings.*

"Since my husband's body is flooded with *feminine* hormones, he understands me much better. He has stopped complaining about my erratic moods and hot flashes because he has them, too.

"Sometimes, we have them in tandem."

Husband Knows Best

Brian, "My wife, Sharon, insisted her nose was too big. I thought she looked great, but she wanted a nose job.

"When she woke up in recovery, Sharon was in a lot of pain. I asked if she needed anything. She said, 'Just get me a casket.'

"I said, 'Well, at least now you can close the lid.'"

The LAUGHING PARTNER

An Aborigine tribe approaches death in a unique way. When someone dies in the village, a special person called the "laughing partner" is sent to the family home. This person's job is to bring joy back to the bereaved.

Meet Laughing Partner
Chaplain Steve Smith.

Steve, "The first thing I do when I walk into a hospital room is say, 'Hi, I'm Steve the chaplain. How are you?' 'Okay,' they usually say. Then I say, 'If you're okay, why are you stuck in the hospital?'

"That joke is usually enough to break the ice. Not always though. Once, I walked into a man's room and tried my 'How's it going?' routine.

"'I'm dying,' he said. This was not the time to kid around. 'Then I will pray God gives you the peace you need.'

"'Teeth?' he said. 'Who said anything about needing teeth? I don't need teeth.' The man was hard of hearing. We both got tickled.

"Another time, a woman was refusing to be admitted to the hospital.

"She said, 'I don't want to stay here. I want to go home.'

"Putting my hand on her shoulder I said, 'I'm the hospital chaplain. When people talk about going home, I wonder what "home" they mean.'

"Laughing, she said, 'I'll check in.'"

"Cancer didn't stop me from being funny. Laughter cut through the tension.

"The first time my brother visited me in the hospital, I was explaining my prostate exam. He was uncomfortable.

"'Wow! My first prostate! Are they supposed to use a puppet?'"

"Part of surviving cancer comes down
Fear is what sets us

"After my fourth surgery, the simplest touch would send my foot twitching out of control. For fun, I'd show people.

"'Watch this!' (Letting my foot go crazy.)

"I was like a kid with a new toy."

"Once you see the profound seriousness in life,

"I was convincing a friend there was such a thing as nasal therapy.

"'As you drink a glass of milk, the doctor makes you laugh and the tumor shoots out through your nose. They're still testing to see if skim and 2% will work.'"

to fear and learning how to handle it.
off in search of humor."

Scott Burton, Cancer Survivor

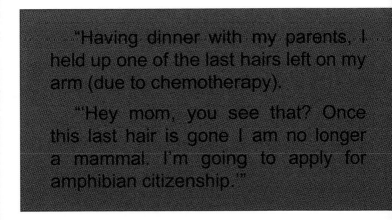

"Having dinner with my parents, I held up one of the last hairs left on my arm (due to chemotherapy).

"'Hey mom, you see that? Once this last hair is gone I am no longer a mammal. I'm going to apply for amphibian citizenship.'"

you can truly recognize the beauty of humor."

BOO

Lloyd, "I was in the hospital with an abscessed pancreas and a temperature of 104. The doctor said I was going to be fine. Later, I overheard him telling my family I might not make it. I was furious.

"The next time I heard the doctor coming down the hall, I pulled the sheet over my head. The doc walked in. I heard him gasp. My plan worked. He thought I was dead. As he pulled the sheet back, I yelled, 'BOO!'

"I got him.

"After we laughed, I insisted he be honest with me and get down to the business of making me feel better."

HELP

Walter Bemak ruptured a disk in his lower back and was paralyzed from the waist down. He lay in the hospital for two weeks waiting for test results.

Walter, "That left me lying flat on my back in bed, unable to go anywhere, and under strict orders not to move under any circumstances. I also was blessed with the unbridled joy of a catheter.

"One night, heavily medicated, I was hallucinating. I had been captured by the Germans during WWII and was being transported in a truck. In the dream, I was climbing over the wooden barriers on the side of the truck.

"I was really climbing over the guardrail of my hospital bed. I woke on the floor, all kinds of tubes sticking out of me, paralyzed from the waist down, yelling for help.

"A nurse came into the room and started shouting. And what does she yell? Code Blue? Emergency? No. She calls out,

"'Don't let anybody come in! He's naked!'"

DUDE LOOKS LIKE A LADY

Jane, "Dad had emergency by-pass surgery. Our family was on pins and needles. My 38-year-old sister died of colon cancer a year before. The thought of losing dad, too, was unbearable.

"The nurse told us dad made it through the operation just fine. She took us to intensive care and pointed to dad's bed.

"He was unrecognizable. His teeth were out; he was smothered in medical equipment. Add to that, bypass patients are usually swollen after surgery. It was hard to believe I was comforting my own father.

"More family members arrived. We bowed our heads, praying for dad's recovery. At that sacred moment, an ICU nurse quietly told us that the person we were praying for was not our father. He was on the other side of the room."

The person they were calling "daddy" was an 85-year-old woman.

THE GREAT PIZZA CAPER

Nan Marr contracted Addison's disease. She lost all use of her legs. The disease moved upwards, immobilizing her from the neck down.

Nan, "When the doctor said I would never walk again, I laughed at him. I refused to accept his diagnosis. I stayed in physical therapy for hours and hours. Even when I would fall down or didn't think I could go on, I made myself have fun.

"One time, the patients on my floor decided to get pizza. The hospital had us on strict diets. We didn't care.

"First, we distracted the nurses. A paralyzed guy dialed the pizza shop using a pencil in his mouth. Next, we assembled a team to meet the delivery man downstairs.

"The team included me, in a wheelchair; Bob, also in a wheelchair; Mary Ann, a dwarf with stubs for legs; and Jeff, paralyzed from the waist down.

"It was a 30-minute delivery and it took us that long to sneak downstairs. When the man arrived, I told him to put all six pizzas on my lap. He said they would burn me. I laughed, explaining I was paralyzed from the waist down.

"Getting back upstairs was more difficult than getting down, since we now had pizza and sodas to contend with. As the elevator climbed, we got excited. Our plan was working. We were home free. Then, the elevator doors opened to a bunch of scowling nurses.

"They took our pizza and sodas then scolded us like children. One yelled, 'You are all grounded!'

"'Grounded?' I laughed. 'We're paralyzed!'

"If I hadn't kept finding humor, I'd still be in a wheelchair."

Get what?

Pam, "My husband Tab, or 'heart-less bastard' as I affectionately call him, was complaining about vertigo. He was throwing up a lot, too. The doctor prescribed a suppository.

"'Suppository?' Tab said. 'I'm not having trouble at that end.'

"It turns out Tab had a stroke. The doctor said that a hole in Tab's heart allowed a blood clot to reach his brain. My husband had a heart after all. We'd have to change his nickname.

"Laughing at being sick is something my grandma taught me. She had a double mastectomy. The hospital gave her a special bra. She called the bra, 'my boobs.'

"I will never forget the first time grandma yelled, 'Pam, I'm going to the store.

Get me my boobs.'

"She wouldn't go anywhere without them, no matter what.

"Even when my grandpa — her husband — was rushed to the emergency room, grandma insisted we stop by the house first to 'pick up her boobs.'"

Injury

Humor was our sanity

Ken, "In Vietnam, sanity was the most important thing we had. To keep it, we had to laugh.

"One of my buddies got his leg blown off during combat. As we put him on the medical helicopter, he said, 'Now I can go home and kick some prosthetic "ass."'

"Now that's funny."

Hunk-a-Hunk Of ...

Terry, "I was trucking down the highway in my old VW van. In my rear-view mirror, I saw there was fire coming out of the back engine. I knew it was in the fuel line. I had to put the fire out before I became a moving fireball."

His car blew up. Three months later he came out of a coma. Terry lay in the hospital with third-degree burns over 60% of his body.

Terry, "I told people I got drunk and fell asleep in a tanning booth or I was a tour guide at Chernobyl.

"My favorite t-shirt I always wear reads ...

'I'm a hunk-a-hunk of burning love.'"

Pass it on

Charley Plumb was a prisoner of war in Vietnam for over 2,700 days. Charley was tortured and nearly beaten to death for information. Sometimes he was beaten because his captors got drunk and thought it was fun.

The first time he was tortured, Charley lay on the cold concrete floor, barely able to open his eyes. Before he passed out from the excruciating pain, he smiled. Scrawled along the bottom of a wall he saw:

"Smile! You're on Candid Camera!"

FORE

Jack Newton was a professional golfer before he was hit by the whirling propeller of a Cessna 210. He lost his right arm, right eye and half his stomach. Jack is now a writer for Australian Golf Digest magazine.

Jack, "Writing is a tough, time consuming craft, especially when you have a glass and cigarette in your only hand."

Chris to Swiss

Chris Bailey was being a Good Samaritan. He picked up three hitchhikers outside a water park in Orlando, Florida.

Chris, "We were laughing and having a good time, so I offered to take them all the way to Daytona.

"A loud bang went off.

"Immediately, one of them wrapped something around my neck, cutting off my air supply. The guy in the front seat started steering toward the side of the road. We rolled to a stop.

"One of the guys in the back got in the driver's side, pushing me to the center of the front seat. Another slapped handcuffs on me. They drove into a marshy, wooded area. The car stopped.

"I remembered I had a knife under the seat. I grabbed it before they got me out of the car. One of them started pulling me into the woods and I stabbed his butt. With my adrenaline raging — I broke the handcuffs and pounced on him.

"Somebody jumped on my back. It felt like I was being punched.

"Actually, I was being stabbed — 16 times.

"I could struggle no more. They covered me with swamp brush and tree branches, leaving me to die. Losing so much blood, I was barely conscious. I could hear the car start.

"I thought my life was over.

"Then I heard it. The car was stuck in the mud. That made me laugh. The thought of those three jerks panicking because they were stuck in a mud hole made me laugh even harder. My laughter was distracting me from the pain. They finally drove away.

"I freed myself from the pile of brush and tree branches. Walking to the road, I kept telling myself to *'keep moving'* and *'keep laughing.'*

"I was found unconscious and taken to a hospital. The three criminals were caught and surprised to find out I was alive to identify them. After months of recovery, I went back to work.

"At first, people didn't know how to act around me. I told them being stabbed 16 times, I went from 'Chris' to 'Swiss.' When they felt more comfortable, people made up their own nicknames: 'Slash' and 'Stick.'"

Oh hell ...

W. Mitchell's motorcycle collided with a laundry truck. When the cycle went down, it crushed his elbow and fractured his pelvis. The gas tank ruptured and the leaking gasoline ignited, burning over 64 percent of his body.

Mitchell's face was burned beyond recognition. His fingers were charred and twisted. His legs were nothing but raw, red flesh. Some visitors, seeing him for the first time, fainted. Mitchchell was unconscious for two weeks.

In the next four months, he had 13 transfusions, 16 skin grafts and numerous surgeries.

Mitchell, "My plastic surgeon was talking to me about my face. He asked if I had a picture of myself before the accident. I gave him my driver's license. The doctor studied it, looked at me and said, 'Oh, hell Mitch, I can do better than that.'"

Dance partner

Sheila's leg was severed when a drunk driver hit her car. Despite wearing a prosthesis, she still plays softball and goes dancing.

Sheila has fun with her fake limb. Every Halloween, she turns it backwards and dresses it up with different shoes.

One time, Sheila and her girlfriend, Gerry, were at a nightclub. They noticed a guy strutting like God's gift to women. This guy was obnoxiously drunk — asking every woman in the bar to dance.

They all turned him down, but Mr. Wonderful wouldn't take no for an answer. He made a second round, hitting on women who had already rejected him.

The second time he came on to Sheila, she took off her leg and waved it in his face, *"Does it look like I want to dance!"*

He left the club mumbling to himself.

From the thoughts of
David Naster

Humor keeps
us flexible

Lucky day

John Ferrintino and his four-year-old son, Jonathan, were on their first fishing trip. Dad was showing his son how to put a worm on the hook. The boy cut his finger and started crying.

John, "I quickly made up a story to distract my son, 'When a fisherman cuts his finger and draws blood, it gives him good luck.'

"With that, Jonathan threw out his line and immediately caught a fish! I looked to the sky and knew there was a God.

"Excited by his catch, Jonathan quickly put another worm on the hook and cut another finger — drawing even more blood.

"Through his tears, he said, 'Wow, daddy! I'm really having a lucky day!'"

Seriously

Bob Weiland got his legs blown off in the Vietnam War. It didn't stop him. He walked across the United States on his arms and butt. Bob started in 1982, finishing in 1986 — three years, eight months and six days later.

People Magazine honored Bob as one of it's Most Amazing Americans. He is a former strength coach for the Green Bay Packers. He was the world record holder in the bench press, once lifting 507 pounds.

Bob has competed in the Ironman Triathlon: a two-mile ocean swim, followed by a 112-mile bicycle ride and a 26-mile run. It took Bob three days without sleep, but he finished.

He was asked if humor helped him with his many challenges. With his trademark smirk,

Bob, "You know, I never took it too seriously that I lost my legs."

Bullet Head

A disgruntled co-worker shot **Traci Riehle** three times.

Husband Tom, "To this day, I call my wife 'Bullet Head.' During her months of recovery, we had fun.

"When a television station asked for a picture of Traci, I gave them one of her in a tutu. When I visited Traci in the hospital and told her about the picture, all of her monitors went off — making lots of noise. The nurses rushed in, finding us both in hysterics.

"Whenever we get into an argument I say, 'They should have kept your jaw wired shut.'"

Traci snaps back, "My voice is like a symphony to you and you know it!!"

Somebody Slap Him

Ginny Klempnauer slammed her Honda CRX into a double-semi rig attempting an illegal U-turn.

Ginny, "When the paramedics put me in the ambulance, one of them asked if anybody knew my weight and age.

"I said, 'Somebody slap him. You don't ask a lady her weight and age. I don't care what condition she's in.'

"The paramedic said, 'We've got a live one here.'

"'Yes you do,' I said, 'and let's keep it that way!'"

Ginny was in ICU for four days with multiple skull fractures, hearing loss, blood clots in her lungs, a broken leg, crushed ankle, constant headaches, double vision, and two knees needed replacing.

"I wore an eye-patch. It scared kids until I told them was a pirate. I was determined not to let the accident turn me into a bitter, shriveled-up person who hates life. I held parties with nurses in my hospital room, from 1:00 to 3:00 a.m. The comedy channel was always on.

"Once, my daughter was in my hospital room when the physical therapist came in to start treatments. He referred to the triangle contraption above my bed. It was there so I could get myself in and out of bed.

"The therapist said, 'I want to concentrate on things you can use in your home to help you maneuver.'

"Before he could say another word, I said, *'Oh, I have much better things than this in my bedroom.'*

"The therapist loved it. My daughter got so embarrassed she left the room."

Damned if I know

Marine Captain Orson Swindle's tour of duty was over. He had completed 205 Combat missions and was due to leave Vietnam in five days. He received a call from operations. They were hurting for pilots. He took one more mission. Captain Swindle was shot down and captured.

He was interrogated and tortured for several weeks during a long march to Hanoi. After arriving, he was called for his initial interrogation at the "Hanoi Hilton," an infamous POW camp. The interrogator, apparently less than experienced, began, 'Are you Air Force?'

'No.'

'Are you Navy?'

'No.'

'Are you Army!?'

'No.'

Totally frustrated, the interrogator screamed, ' Why are you here!?!'

'Damned if I know. I've been trying to figure that out for the last four weeks!'

That was not what the interrogator wanted to hear.

C**aptain Swindle,** "The look on the guy's face was worth the punishment."

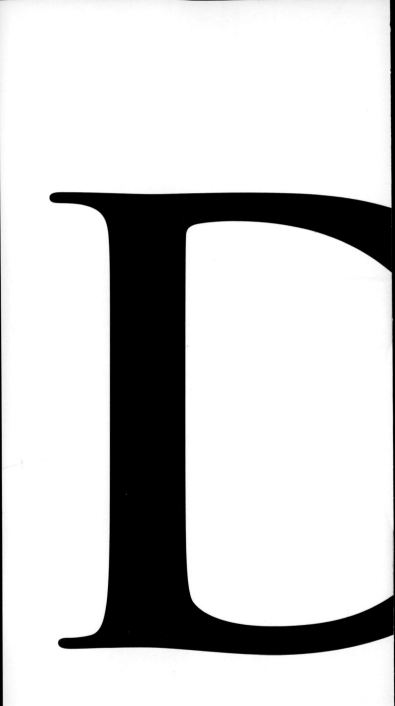

anger

BATS ON A SUBWAY

A comedian finished a late-night comedy set in midtown New York City. He had another show in Greenwich Village. A cab would cost him nearly all the money he just made. So, even though it can be dangerous that time of night, the comic took the subway.

He was relieved to find he was the only passenger in his car. That feeling didn't last. Six punk rockers came barging in, laughing and making a lot of noise with their military boots. They wore torn clothing and had multicolored Mohawks. Their faces were pierced like pin cushions.

All carried baseball bats.

The train started moving. The punkers started banging their bats on the floor, seats and windows. When they saw the comedian in the corner, they stopped. They stared at him. The comic broke the silence.

"Big game tonight, fellas?"

They joked all the way downtown.

What Are You Doing?

Vietnam veteran **Larry Marks**, "Oh there were things in Vietnam that were funny. It was always in the middle of something serious.

"We were in a swamp. There were bullets flying in every direction. I wasn't sure we were going to make it. I was really scared.

"I looked over at another soldier. The guy weighed at least 250 pounds. He was sitting in the water, completely covered with frogs and eating a can of peaches.

"I mouthed over to him, *'What are you doing?'*

"He mouthed back, *'I'm hungry.'*"

STOCK UP ON CANNED GOODS

In Bay City, Michigan, a woman was working the midnight shift at a convenience store. A man entered and wandered around for over 30 minutes. The clerk got frightened, worrying the man was going to rob her.

He approached, setting a can of pork and beans on the counter. Relieved, the clerk turned around to ring up the sale. When she turned back, the man had exposed himself — placing "it" on the counter.

Without thinking, she picked up the can of pork and beans and slammed it on his exposed organ. The guy dropped. Slamming his head on the counter, he flopped unconscious on the floor.

The clerk dialed 911 and the police arrived within minutes. The man was arrested once he regained consciousness. Escorting him to the squad car, a policeman said, "I bet you wish you grabbed a loaf of bread instead!"

I KNEW BETTER THAN TO ANSWER

Rich, "I called my pregnant wife. I barely got out, 'Hello,' before she said, 'Call back in 15 minutes. I'm expecting a call from the doctor,' and hung up.

"Fifteen minutes later I found out my adorable wife confused her prenatal pills with our dog, Elroy's, heart worm medication. She accidentally took the dog's pills and called the doctor to see if she or the baby was in danger. The doctor assured her they would both be fine. I asked if she gave Elroy the prenatal pills. She said,

"'What do you think I am, stupid?'"

Laugh or I'll Shoot

"I teach people to laugh in the middle of fear," begins therapist Jeanene Tichenor.

"I worked with a husband and wife who kept coming in with the same problems. They never followed through with any of the solutions we agreed on. For weeks this went on with no change.

"During one afternoon session, the wife pulled a gun and threatened to shoot her husband. I laughed. The shocked woman asked what was so funny.

"I said, 'You never follow through with anything. I'm sure you won't with this either.'"

Nighty-Night

Richie Minnervini was pulled over by police on Long Island. The cops told Richie to get out of the car and said he fit the description of a wanted drug dealer.

Richie, "First off, I'm no dealer. Second, you can't stop me because you think I'm selling dope. That would be as stupid as arresting me because I'm thinking about punching both of you."

Seconds later, Richie's smart mouth got him handcuffed and headed to jail.

At the detention center, Richie was handed a blanket and pillow. He was taken to a large holding cell filled with some of New York's finest thugs.

Richie returned from making his one phone call to find his pillow and blanket stolen. Mad at himself, nerves rattled, Richie screamed, "Whoever took my blanket and pillow, I want them back. Right now!"

A man the size of a building stepped forward. "I've got what you want. So what are you going to do about it?"

Standing 5'6", maybe 170 pounds, Richie looked up at the man and said, "Give them back now. If you don't, somebody is going to get his butt kicked. And it's probably going to be me."

There was a second of silence before everyone got it. The big guy was the last to get the joke.

"Here's your blanket," he said. "I'm keeping the pillow."

Hit the Highlights

Ernie Stautner is a National Football League Hall-of-Famer. He was known for his toughness.

Ernie, "Pain has always been my friend. I've had broken ribs, a cracked sternum and have broken my nose seven times. My knees were twisted like pretzels. I crushed the carpal tunnel bones in both hands. One game, I broke my thumb. With blood all over my uniform, I stuck the bone back in, walked to the huddle, and casually asked, 'What's the defense for this play?'

"Before a game against the Cleveland Browns, I was mistakenly given Demerol instead of Novocaine; 1,200 milligrams — enough to knock out a horse.

"Four hours later, I couldn't tell if I was awake or dreaming. A nurse was holding an oxygen mask over my mouth shouting,

'Breathe, damn it, breathe!'

"My eyes opened. One of the doctors asked me, *'Do you know who you are?'*

"'Yeah, I think I'm Ernie Stautner.'

"'Do you know what you were supposed to do today?'

"'I was supposed to beat the Browns. But somehow, Doc, I don't think I made it.'

"I saw him go over to a group of physicians. They were whispering. I was sure something was wrong.

"'Give me a priest,' I shouted, then fell asleep. A nurse yelled,

'Breathe, damn it, breathe!'

"A priest arrived and said to me, *'Do you think you are going to die?'*

"'Yes, father. I need to say my last confession. Father bless me, for I have sinned ...'

"I stopped. I was feeling dizzy. The room was starting to move and getting darker.

"I began again, 'Excuse me father. I don't have much time. Is it all right if I just hit the highlights?'"

Come On In

Bob "Woodsy" Woods, a New York comic, had fallen on hard times. He was living in his car. After an evening performance, Woodsy got a ride "home" from his friend, Vinnie.

The temperature was near zero. Vinnie begged Woodsy not to sleep in his car, fearing he would freeze to death. Woodsy said he would be fine.

Vinnie pulled up to the car, pleading with his friend not to risk freezing to death. Woodsy said good night, thanked him for the ride, and went into the frigid night.

Vinnie, "As I drove off, I looked in my rear- view mirror and saw Woodsy frantically waving his arms. He was signaling me to come back. Finally, he was coming to his senses.

"I pulled up. Woodsy gestured for me to roll down the window. He pointed at his car saying, *'How rude of me! Would you like to come in for a while?'*"

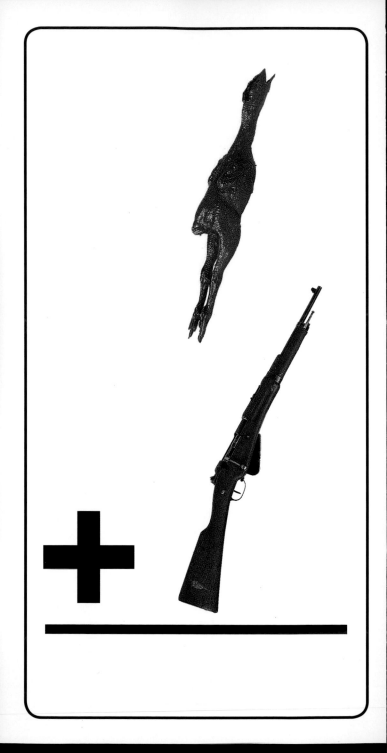

Ready ... Aim ...

Norm Alden, "After one of my late-night comedy shows, I took a waitress friend to her home. She was too drunk to drive.

"At her request, I dropped her off a block from her house. She claimed her husband was a light sleeper and the car noise would wake him up.

"The next afternoon, I was taking a nap outside in a lawn chair. When I woke up, I was staring down the barrel of a shotgun.

"The man holding the gun shouted, 'I know you were with my wife last night! I saw you drop her off! I wondered why she had been coming home late! Now I know!'

"Keeping cool I said, 'Take it easy. I gave your wife a ride home because she was too drunk to drive.'

"The irate husband continued, 'I know you've been sleeping with her! You didn't even have enough guts to drive her to the house! So now I am going to kill everybody! I am going to start with you, then her. Then I am going to finish myself off last!'

"I said, 'Well, that sounds like a plan. But why don't you start with yourself?'

"The husband kept glaring like he hadn't heard a word. Then, he slowly realized what I said and lowered the gun. He laughed. Best laugh I ever got.

"We actually went out and had a beer."

She's a Jamaican

Patrick Murray is a master ventriloquist. He's six-foot, two inches tall, and white. One puppet he uses in his act is a black Jamaican puppet named **Matilda**. Patrick's Jamaican accent is so authentic that Jamaicans enjoy Matilda's character more than anyone.

Patrick, "I was going through customs in Montego Bay to board a cruise ship. A Jamaican official was looking through my bag, saw a couple of the puppet heads and said, *'Oh my God, this is something bad.'*

"I immediately explained I was a ventriloquist. He didn't understand. The official kept searching my bags. I was afraid I might miss my ship or even end up in jail.

"After 20 minutes, I reached into the bag and pulled out Matilda. I put her right in the official's face and said in a perfect Jamaican accent, 'Hello, my darling.'

"The customs official stepped back and said,

'Oh my God, she's Jamaican.'

"Matilda and the customs official started having a conversation — never acknowledging it was me doing the talking. They were becoming fast friends.

"I had Matilda call the customs official closer and whisper, 'See this big, white "mon" behind me? He knows some WICKED VOODOO.'

"I was through customs in seconds."

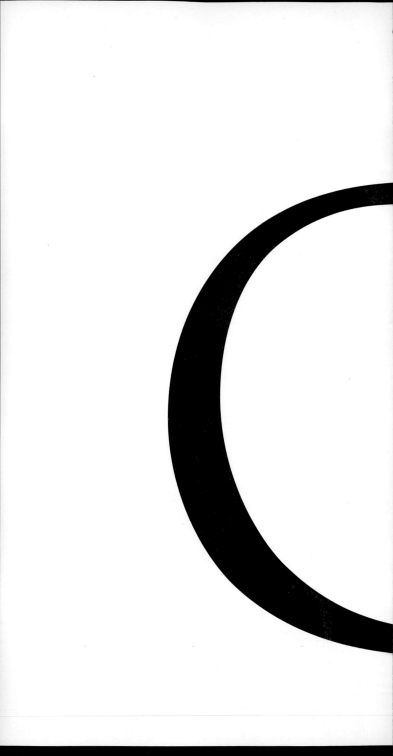

Grief

Pleasant Memories

Rabbi Alan Cohen, "Bringing joy to a grieving family is the perfect gift."

"One man was late his entire life. At his funeral I said, 'Today, he was finally on time.'

"During another service, I said of a woman, 'She would never, ever let me get the last word. Today, I will.'

"In eulogies, I joke about the deceased being a bad cook or wearing socks that don't match.

"I choose my words carefully to evoke a pleasant memory of the departed — not to be a comedian. People in attendance, especially the family, appreciate those funny memories."

Thanks for the Memories

Legendary comedian Bob Hope proved to be funny right up to the end. With not long to live, his wife, Delores, asked him where he would like to be buried.

Bob said, "Surprise me."

Ready – Set – Stop

Nurse Patty,
"I asked a 102-year-old woman if she was afraid to die.

"She said, 'No, I'm ready to go.'

"'Is something stopping you?' I said. 'You know you'll probably meet your late husband.'

"'That's what's stopping me,' she said."

Proper grammar

JIM, "My father, Jay Fussell, was one of the smartest people I'd ever known - and the nicest. My sister, Nancy, and I had our grammar corrected throughout our lives. The reason was dad was an assistant editor for Webster's Third International Dictionary. Words and good grammar were his life.

"You can find his name in the front of the huge book that most people only see in libraries. He had a PhD in the history of religions, spoke several languages, and defined all the religion words in the dictionary.

"Near the end of my Dad's life he had a stroke. Weeks later it looked as if he may pass away. My sister, Nancy, and her husband, John, rushed to dad's side. "In a weak and tremulous voice dad said, 'You didn't have to rush over here.'

"'Don't be silly,' my sister said, 'It was very important to John and I.'

"Weak, and barely able to talk, Dad motioned for Nancy to come closer. When she did, my father whispered, 'To John and me.'

"Nancy laughed and gave him a great big hug. He died shortly thereafter.

"That was Dad to a 'T.' Even on his deathbed, he was concerned about our good grammar.

"Nancy and I have laughed about that for years as we fondly remember our loving and intelligent grammarian of a father."

Humor in Divorce

In the middle of a tense divorce proceeding, the husband returned to the house to pick up the last of his possessions.

Before walking out the front door he turned, looking at his soon-to-be ex-wife.

Man, "I know this has been difficult for you. It's been kind of tough for me, too. After this is all over, do you think we can still have sex?"

She looked at him in amazement.

Woman, "Sure we can. Just not with each other!"

She smiled and shut the door.

EXPIRED

Wendy, "One Sunday night, mom and I were watching TV. The phone rang. Mom answered. She nodded a few times and hung up.

"*'That was Aunt Maude's nursing home,'* mom said. '*The nurse said Maude took a turn for the worse.'*

"'*A turn for the worse?'* I asked. '*What does that mean?'*

"*'The nurse said that Maude expired.'*

"'*Well, that is a turn for the worse,'* I said.

"*'And expired! What is she, milk?'* mom asked.

"It took two seconds before we busted out laughing."

NO GUNS ALLOWED

A 28-year-old man impregnated John's 17-year-old daughter. Against John's wishes, they got married. Two months later, the father-to-be killed himself, like his two older brothers and father did a few years before.

All four men killed themselves with the same gun.

The girl called her dad. Crying, telling him of her husband's suicide, she begged her father to let her come home.
John said, *"Of course you can, honey.*

"But for God's sake, don't bring that gun."

Lifetime Guarantee

Martha Blazek, "A family member named Ken passed away. The family went with Diane, Ken's wife, to the funeral home.

"The funeral director explained that Ken would be buried in a different casket. The one they chose hadn't arrived because Ken died earlier than expected.

"In his most empathetic voice, the funeral director assured Diane the casket was an upgrade. He also said the casket manufacturer would plant a tree in Ken's name. There would be no marker, and the family would never know what kind of tree or where it was planted. We looked at each other, thinking, 'Why even tell us?'

"The director added that the casket had a lifetime guarantee. We looked at each other, mouthing: 'Lifetime guarantee? Whose lifetime?' Seriously, who digs up a casket to see if the 'lifetime guarantee' was good?"

MORNING of MOURNING

Reverend Emmanuel Cleaver, "My mother died in 1986. I have never known that kind of depression. It was the deepest funk I had ever been in. Even as a minister, I kept asking God, 'Why?' Why did He take my mother? I almost gave up the ministry.

"A pastor friend, Howard Creecy, phoned. He offered condolences, then started joking. I never would have believed I could laugh again. After that, humor was a part of every one of my sermons. Like Proverbs states: 'A merry heart doeth good like medicine.'

"Let me give you an example: I was in a hospital room where a woman's father had just died. The woman asked her husband for some money so she could get something to eat.

"I looked at the husband and said, 'When I married the two of you a couple years ago, I thought it would take at least five years before she took all of your money.'

"As it is written in Psalms 30:5: 'Weeping may tarry the night, but joy comes with the morning.' I believe that passage. One day is all people should grieve. Like darkness, pain and misery must end, giving way to light and joy.

"Some say I am irreverent, but I'm willing to violate some 'rules' of mourning to put joy back into people's hearts. I'm not the only one who does this. I sat with Bill Cosby after his son, Ennis, was killed. Bill was making everybody in the room laugh — doing an impression of his minister. It was less than a month after Ennis died and Bill was joking around."

Another Side of Bill Cosby

"Through humor, you can soften the worst blows life delivers. Once you find humor in anything, you can survive it. No matter how painful your situation might be, you can survive."

Bill Cosby said this a year before his son Ennis was murdered. It proved prophetic.

At Ennis' grave, the Cosby family shared stories about Ennis. The tales moved from solemn testimonials to humorous recollections. Their tears turned to smiles.

Bill, "My family walked down the hill to Ennis' grave as slaves to our emotions. After we laughed, we walked up that same hill freer of sadness."

SALE

Nancy, "My best friend, Julie's, brother was very frugal. Sadly, he killed himself.

"A month after the funeral, Julie called. She was laughing. While going over her brother's bills, she found a receipt for the gun he used to kill himself. He charged it.

"And it was on sale."

Go to the Light

Nurse Judy cares for dying patients and counsels families of the terminally ill.

Judy, "Fran had been suffering from a chronic illness for many years. Her daughter, Sue, had been her primary caretaker. Fran was nearing the end so I sat down to prepare Sue for her mom's death.

"We discussed the importance of saying good-bye, offering forgiveness and giving her mom permission to die.

"I told Sue, 'When your mom is ready, tell her to go toward the light.'

"Fran's vitals were diminishing rapidly, but she would not let go. Sue was exhausted and emotionally drained.

"One evening, I heard whispering in Fran's room. I peeked in. Sue was shining a flashlight on the ceiling, whispering to her mother, 'Go to the light. Go to the light.'

"I ran away snorting."

The BS Card

A humor expert spoke at a national meeting of homicide detectives. He made the statement, "It is possible to find humor in anything."

After the show, a detective approached the speaker and said, "During your little talk I wanted to stand up and play the bullshit card. You said you can find humor in anything? Tell me this — what is funny about a 17-year-old kid getting killed in a car wreck?"

"I don't know," the speaker said.

"You're damn right you don't know. My 17-year-old son, Adam, was killed in a car wreck that wasn't his fault. I didn't interrupt your talk because I'm a gentleman.

"But as I came down to throw the bullshit card in your face, it hit me. You are right.

"After my son's funeral, we had the entire family over. We had hamburgers, tacos and fried chicken. Looking around, I had the feeling my son was speaking through me. Getting everyone's attention, I said, 'If Adam was here, he'd say, "Dad, did I have to die for you to finally get all my favorite fast foods at one time?"'

"Everyone laughed. So did I, through my tears. It's true. You can find humor in anything. *Thank you for reminding me.*"

Kickin' Ash

Beverly **Jamison,** "When my sister Shirley died, my brother Warren and I decided to spread her ashes on the farm where we were born. As we scattered her remains over a meadow of wildflowers, a lump fell to the ground.

"Warren kicked it, saying, 'There you go sis, one last kick in the ash.'

"We laughed so hard we had to hang on to each other so we wouldn't fall over. Shirley would have loved it."

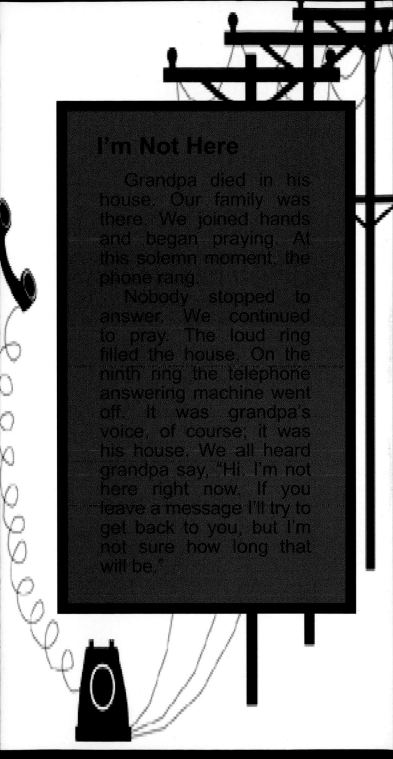

I'm Not Here

Grandpa died in his house. Our family was there. We joined hands and began praying. At this solemn moment, the phone rang.

Nobody stopped to answer. We continued to pray. The loud ring filled the house. On the ninth ring the telephone answering machine went off. It was grandpa's voice, of course; it was his house. We all heard grandpa say, "Hi. I'm not here right now. If you leave a message I'll try to get back to you, but I'm not sure how long that will be."

More from
CHAPLAIN SMITH

Steve, "It's okay to have fun at funerals. After all, the first three letters of funeral are f-u-n.

"A woman insisted on being cremated. She wanted her ashes spread on her vegetable garden, just so I would say at her funeral,

'She was one hot tomato.'

"At another funeral, the family made a picture board of their departed husband and father. One photo showed him dancing with his wife. Thank goodness you're Methodist,' I said. 'If you were Baptist, he wouldn't get into heaven.'

"At another memorial service, I began, 'Our lost loved one, Jack, is still with us today. Right here, right now.' Pointing at the casket, I said, 'And I'm not talking about Jack-in-the-box.'

"The family was stunned — then started laughing. The widow turned to Jack's brother and said, 'Tell him.'

"Jack's brother stood. 'Several months ago, Jack was at the funeral of a friend named Bob.

"During the ceremony, Jack whispered, 'There's my buddy. He's Bob-in-a-box. One day, they'll say the same about me. "There's Jack-in-the-box.'"

"One of the funniest moments ever was at a woman's funeral. The deceased wrote her own eulogy and asked that a special song be played.

"Reading the glowing eulogy, I noticed many in attendance giving each other puzzled looks. Apparently, the dearly departed wasn't as wonderful as she thought.

"At the eulogy's conclusion I said, 'And here's how she wished to be remembered.'

"At that sensitive moment, 'Somewhere Over the Rainbow' from 'The Wizard of Oz' was suppose to play. **'Ding Dong the Witch is Dead'** came over the sound system instead."

Funny Side of Suicide

Randy, "I attempted to kill myself several times. This last time, I saw Jesus. He told me to go back. It wasn't my time yet.

"The funny thing is, I'm Jewish.

"Since that moment, I find humor everywhere. It gets me through the day."

Sarah decided to end her life. She parked her car in the garage, closed the door and left the motor running.

Sarah, "The next morning, I woke up realizing I was still alive. Not only that, I was out of gas.

"While walking to the service station, I realized that the good Lord must want me to stick around."

Deb Anthony
Hospice Nurse

Deb, "Hospice humor? You've got to be kidding! What could you laugh at in a hospice? Death and dying? That's serious stuff. But you learn to laugh.

"You laugh with a co-worker who complained about a foul odor and later found a dead mouse in her pocket — put there by a patient as a practical joke.

"You laugh at a teaching session demonstrating proper procedure for changing a roll of toilet paper.

"You learn laughter relieves pain like medication, but with far fewer side effects.

"You learn laughter adds life to the days of a dying patient.

"You learn the most deadly of all life-threatening conditions is the absence of laughter. Yet, this condition is curable, simply by learning to laugh."

> ## "My dad's last two weeks were the best two weeks of my life."
>
> Johnny Rowlands

Johnny, "Dad was bedridden. He said he would love a long, hot shower.

"I started the shower. By the time I got back to the bedroom, dad was laughing. He was sitting on the edge of the bed, totally naked.

"He said to me, 'Whoever thought I'd end up looking like this? My nipples are below my knees.'

"I put dad in the wheelchair. We started toward the shower. He reminded me I would have to help him in the shower. I took off my clothes.

"There we were, father and son, naked — making our way through the living room. As we passed by the front door, a cousin knocked and walked right in.

"'*Anybody home?*' she called.

"Then she saw us. We all froze. She stared. We stared.

"'*This isn't a good time,*' she said. '*I'll come back.*'

"She left.

"We couldn't quit laughing.

"The family gathered around dad's bed. The time was near. Looking around the room, a gentle smile crawled across dad's face. Soon he was beaming.

"'Look at all of you,' he said. 'What a wonderful family ... .'

"Then he got serious.

"'I'm ready to go, but I don't know how to open the door.'

"'Don't worry dad,' I said. 'Go whenever you want. Selfishly, we want you to stay. But you go whenever you are ready.'

Silence.

"'Is there anything we can get you? Is there anything you want?'

"The whole family watched, wondering what he might ask for.

"'O'Doul's ...,' he said softly. 'I would like an O'Doul's.'

"I said, 'You want a non-alcoholic beer?'

"'The doctor said I shouldn't have anything with booze in it.'

"We all laughed, but he was serious. He wanted that O'Douls.

"As he drank through a straw, dad started cracking jokes.

"'Before you pull the sheet over me, make sure I'm dead. And when you cremate me, make sure I don't have a pulse before you stick me in there.'

"That was dad. He loved making people laugh — all the way to the end."

PUMP IT UP

James Johann, "A porcelain-skinned redhead with sparkling Hollywood eyes gave my heart a sucker punch it didn't deserve. She cheated on me with a **hunky** bodybuilder.

"I have always been on the puny side. Getting dumped for 'Fabio' made me feel even more inadequate.

"It was time for a change.

"I drove home from the health store with a $50 jar of muscle-building powder. I knew that if I followed a strict diet and exercise regimen, I would have the body to win her back.

"I poured a giant glass of milk to mix with the muscle powder. Ten minutes later, I was still trying to get the lid off the muscle mix.

"My face turned red. A vein on my forehead was the size of a garden hose. My arms shook violently as I twisted and turned, trying desperately to get that stupid lid off. When I was on the floor, wrestling with that jar of muscle powder, it happened.

"I laughed. I was actually fighting an inanimate object — and it was winning. Now, the thought of 'winning her back' with a muscle-man body was hysterical. I saved that jar of powder. It reminds me to laugh.

"I still can't open it."

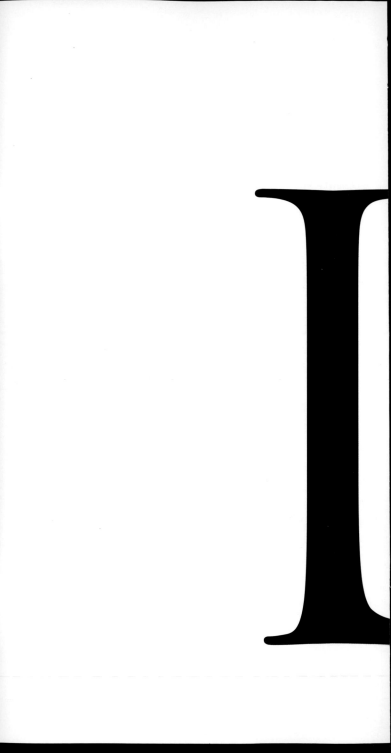

How Laughter Happens

Dr. Peter Derks, "Laughing in response to something funny is a sophisticated brain function. About four-tenths of a second after we hear a punch line of a joke, before we laugh, a negatively charged wave of electricity sweeps through the entire cerebral cortex. All or most of the higher brain plays a role. The left hemisphere works on the joke's verbal content while the analytic right hemisphere figures out the incongruity. When our brain 'gets' the connection, we laugh."

Humor

is Physical

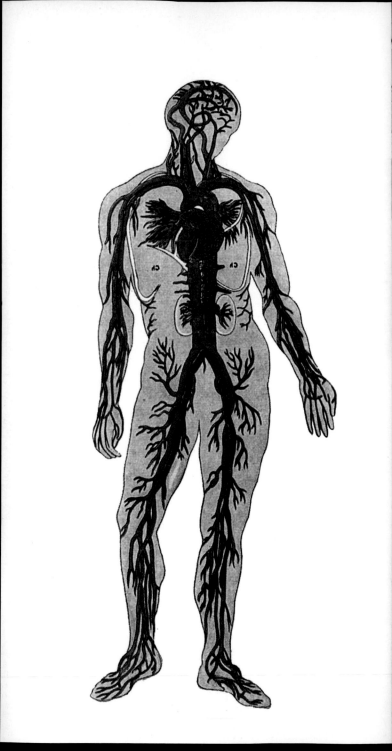

The physical act of laughing has serious health benefits.

Dr. Michael Miller is the Director for the Center of Preventive Cardiology at the University of Maryland Medical Center.

Dr. Miller, "The old saying that 'laughter is the best medicine' appears to be true when it comes to protecting your heart. Mental stress is associated with impairment of the endothelium, the protective barrier lining our blood vessels. This can cause a series of inflammatory reactions that lead to fat and cholesterol build-up in the coronary arteries and ultimately to a heart attack.

"Laughter, along with an active sense of humor, may help protect you against a heart attack.

"People with heart disease are less likely to recognize humor or use it to get out of uncomfortable situations. They generally laughed less even in positive situations. They displayed more anger and hostility.

"The ability to laugh — either naturally or as a learned behavior, may have important implications in societies such as the U.S. where heart disease remains the number one killer.

"Exercising, not smoking and eating foods low in saturated fat will reduce the risk of heart disease. Regular, hearty laughter should be added to the list."

Pain-Free

Norman Cousins was diagnosed with a terminal illness. Cousins was given only a year to live. Thanks to his discovery that laughter is an integral part of the healing process, he lived for 15 more years.

Norman, "I made the joyous discovery that 10 minutes of genuine belly laughter had an anesthetic effect and would give me at least *two hours of pain-free sleep.*

"I call laughing 'inner jogging.' When we engage in a good hearty laugh, every system in our body gets a workout.

"I see *humor as food.* An adequate share of humor and laughter represents an essential part of the diet of the healthy person."

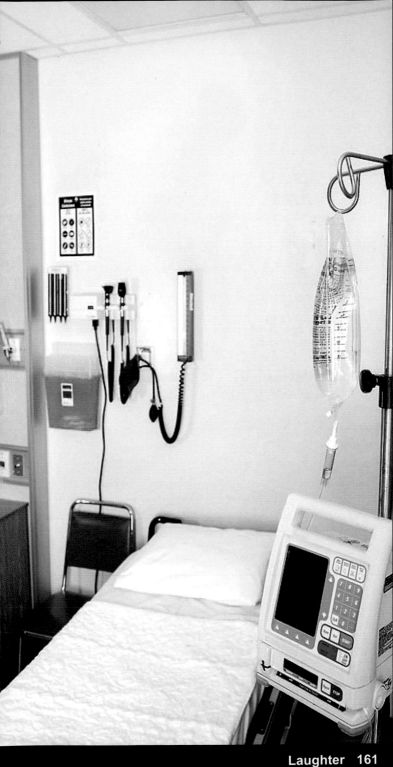

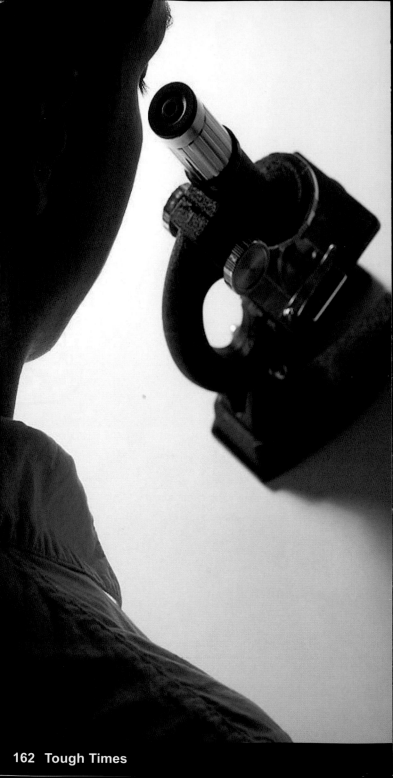

Immune System

In the 1980 *New England Journal of Medicine*, **Dr. Franz Ingelfinger** estimated that 85% of all human illnesses can be cured by systems already present in our bodies.

For example, there is a healing agent called Immunoglobulin A, produced by our immune system. These IgA cells are the body's first line of defense. They attack foreign organisms, protect us from respiratory problems and have proven to destroy tumor cells and viruses.

The presence of IgAs varies according to our moods. People with a well-developed sense of humor have been proven to have increased concentrations of IgAs. Watching a one-hour humorous video increases the activity of these natural healing cells.

The American Journal of Medical Sciences, December 1989, states there is a direct connection between stress, high blood pressure, muscle tension, and immunosuppression, the inhibition of the immune response.

Laughter stimulates the immune system, off-setting the effects of stress by lowering serum cortisol levels and increasing the amount of activated T lymphocytes. The layman's interpretation?

Laughter heals.

IT GETS BETTER

Herbert Lefcourt, Ph.D.
"Laughter helps us contend with the unthinkable — our mortality. People's willingness to sign an organ donor card rises with their tendency to laugh. Very few people are ready to think, even for a moment, about death. Those who have a sense of humor are more able to cope with the idea."

Dr. Joseph Richman, Psychiatrist
"Laughter counteracts feelings of alienation, a major factor in depression and suicide. In a study of depressed and suicidal senior citizens, the patients who recovered were the ones who demonstrated a sense of humor."

John Morreall, Ph.D.
"After you laugh, you go into a relaxed state. Laughter also helps us think more creatively. Humor loosens up the mental gears. It encourages out-of-the-ordinary ways of looking at things."

40 Years of Research

Dr. William Fry, "Laughing has an immediate impact on the body. The brain is stimulated into greater alertness, enhancing memory and sociability. Laughter increases the concentration of antibodies circulating in the blood stream.

"A person who laughs a lot is more resistant to developing infection and other illnesses.

"The stimulation of laughter increases our circulation — benefitting the heart and lowering blood pressure. Laughter increases our respiratory exchange. It also increases our metabolism and activity of our muscles.

"Laughing for 20 seconds gives the body the kind of workout you would get from 3 minutes of rigorous exercise."

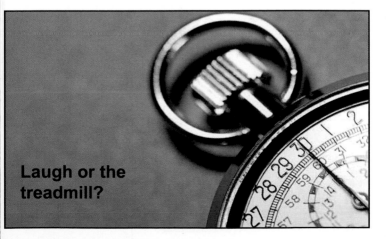

Laugh or the treadmill?

**Laugh
like
your
life
depends
on
it.**

It does.

I trust the true stories you just read made you laugh — hopefully out loud. It is my sincerest wish that this guidebook helps you get through any tough time.

Live Amused!
David

Latest Release

This guidebook offers a sincere and humorous insight on how healthcare professionals and families appreciate the gift of laughter when dealing with death.

A special thanks to all of those who graciously contributed their most personal experiences and humorous insights.

2008 AATH*
Humor Book Award Winner

This guidebook has three goals. The first is to make you laugh. The second is to teach you how to find humor. The third is to improve your work life.

* Association of Applied Therapeutic Humor

DAVID NASTER

When Work Gets
TOUGH

YOU
JUST
HAVE
TO

LAUGH

A GUIDEBOOK

NASTER.COM

PRESENTATIONS
BOOKS
DVD